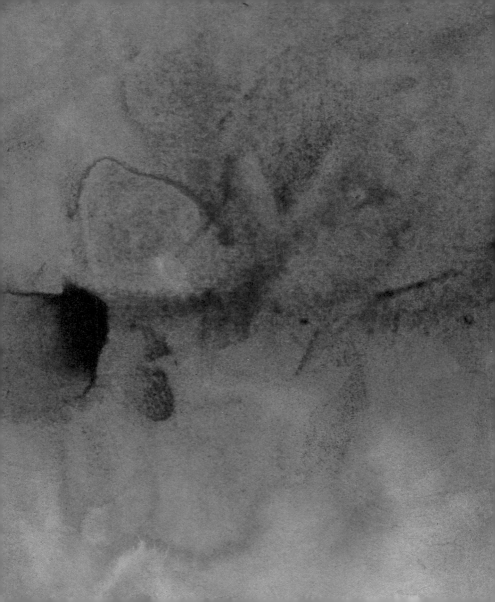

KIRSTEN BURKE'S

LITTLE BOOK OF

Calming

CALLIGRAPHY

**STUDIO
PRESS**

Hello!

I'm Kirsten Burke and I've been a professional calligrapher for 20 years! In this time, I've been creating artworks using the most awe-inspiring wording, whether it be simple messages of love from one person to another, or famous quotes from poets, philosophers and world leaders. As I write, I focus on each letter and the rhythmic strokes of my calligraphy, and my mood lifts.

Calligraphy is the perfect escape. You become completely absorbed in what you're doing, forgetting about everything else.

In this book, I've put together some of my favourite quotes and phrases, as they remind me to cherish the moment. I hope they'll help you to zone out and become inspired by the words you're writing!

New to Modern Calligraphy?

If you've never used a nib or brush before, you'll need to pick up a copy of my nib book, *Secrets of Modern Calligraphy*, or my brush book, *Secrets of Brush Calligraphy*. Both are available from most high-street and online retailers. In them, I guide you through the basic skills you need and give you all my expert tips, to help make learning calligraphy easier and a lot more fun!

How to Use This Book

This book is designed for you to be able to 'dip' into whenever you need to relax, if you'll forgive the pun.

I start off with a quick recap on the basics of modern calligraphy and some simple warm-up exercises, followed by templates for you to trace. Before some of the more challenging templates I have provided further tips and advice to help you complete the exercises to the best of your ability.

15 minute chill-out

We've included timing prompts to help you to choose which quote to work on, depending on how long you've got. They're just a guide – there are no right or wrongs – it's all about relaxing and enjoying yourself. The options you will find to choose from are:

Take 5 • 10-minute time out • 15-minute chill-out • 20-minute tea break • 25-minute zone out • 30-minute focus

Troubleshooting

As you work your way through the book, you'll come across tips and advice for improving certain skills. These are designed to help you with some of the more common problems that you might encounter, or to teach you a new skill to be used on the following pages.

On some pages I've created simple shapes and drills for you to zone out to. These exercises will help you practise your thick and thin letter strokes, so that your calligraphy improves as you work through them.

I've divided the quotes up according to the time it takes to complete an exercise so that, whether you have a quick five minutes to spare while you're making a cup of tea, or you're able to sit down for an hour and really immerse yourself, you'll find something to suit you.

Challenges

If you've already done quite a bit of calligraphy, or would like to push yourself further, look out for the 'Challenge' icon. Wherever you see it, you can make the project on that page more difficult by following the instructions. The challenges are optional, so there's no pressure to make it harder if you don't want to or if your time is limited. Choose whatever makes you feel comfortable! If you love the challenge, why not try using the same technique on some of the other pages?

Go it Alone

Here and there, I invite you to spend time writing and practising your own choice of letters or words, so just enjoy this free working space. Some people find a blank page a little scary. If this is the case, use these pages to just doodle away. Or, it might be that you've had trouble with a particular combination of letters that you can practise here and repeat. For more of a challenge, try copying the quote on the opposite page as closely as you can, without any guidelines to trace over. You may like to sketch the quote out in pencil first.

Nib or Brush?

The templates in this book are designed at the correct scale for a pointed nib, but a *small* brush pen will also work. Brush pens are handy, as you can take them anywhere and you also don't need a bottle of ink.

You could use a nib when you're at home and a brush pen when you're on the move.

YouTube
Kirsten Burke Calligraphy
Brush Secrets – Types of brush pen

Brush Pens

The difference between brush pens and felt-tip markers is that brush pens have a flexible tip that behaves in a similar way to a paintbrush. When you apply pressure to the paper, you can create the same thick or thin lines as you can with a nib.

I recommend...

Kirsten Burke Sailor Pen
It has two sizes of brush tip: one small, one large. It gives a very satisfying solid black and the two sizes of brush means you can work at different scales with just one pen.

Pentel Fude Touch Sign Pen
This small brush pen has a crisp feel, it's easy to control and as well as black, it also comes in vivid colours. They're water-based, so you can colour blend with these.

Pointed Nibs

A pointed nib is made up of two split pieces of metal that fit perfectly together. These are called the 'tines'. The tines lead to a small hole called a 'vent', which holds the ink. The tines must open up as you write to allow the ink or paint to flow.

Before you dip your nib into the ink, place the tip of it flat on the paper then, as you apply pressure, you'll see them open up. The more they open, the thicker your stroke will be.

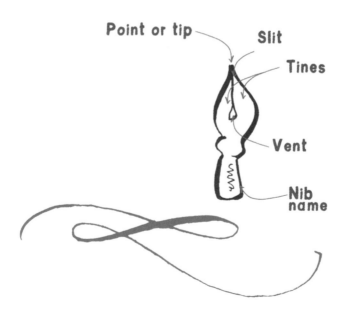

Point or tip
Slit
Tines
Vent
Nib name

Seasoning

Nibs have a glaze on them. It not only protects them from rusting, but it also repels the ink, so you need to remove it. Just hold the nib over a flame for a few seconds, as if you were sterilising a needle. This is called 'seasoning'.

Fitting a Nib

Push the nib firmly into the side of the four 'petals', against the inside rim of the penholder as far as it'll go until it feels secure.

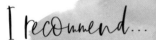

Leonardt 30 Pointed Nib
This is the most popular nib by far in my workshops. It provides great ink flow, and is flexible enough to make those thick and thin lines easily.

Leonardt 33 and the Principle EF Nib
These are wonderful if you're more experienced and want to try a more delicate nib.

YouTube
Kirsten Burke Calligraphy
Secrets – Nibs

What Makes it Modern?

It's all about lettering that has energy and flow. While it's important that the lettering is balanced on the page, each individual letter doesn't need to be identical every time. It's about creating lettering that looks human and that has personality.

Modern calligraphy encourages you to play with the traditional rules, but it still takes patience to learn. Like most skills, it doesn't happen overnight, so remember whenever you practise to experiment, changing the pressure and release to get thick and thin strokes. That way you'll be a fabulous modern calligrapher before you know it.

How is Modern Calligraphy Different from Traditional Calligraphy?

The key to modern calligraphy is that it's written with a pointed nib or pointed brush. The thick and thin lines are made by pressing down harder and softer as you go up and down. Traditional calligraphy uses a nib with a wide, flat end called a 'broad edged nib', which you hold at a consistent angle in order to create the thick and thin strokes of your lettering.

Page Position

Turn the book 40 degrees anticlockwise if you are right-handed.
Clockwise for lefties. Aim the pen, nib and page so that they all follow
the same direction, because then the nib can open up and give you a
thick line as you pull it downwards.

Move the book if you feel you need to, in order to get your pen into
the position you need when working on more elaborate designs. You
want the pen's tines to be able to separate easily on the downstroke,
as the wider they split open the thicker your line will be.

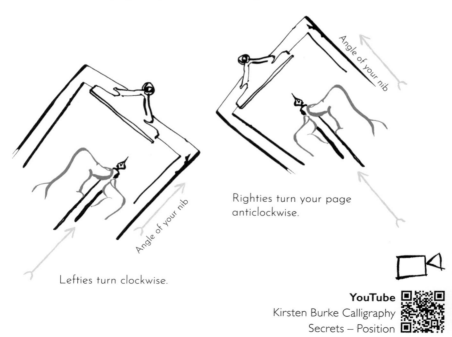

Angle of your nib

Righties turn your page
anticlockwise.

Angle of your nib

Lefties turn clockwise.

YouTube
Kirsten Burke Calligraphy
Secrets – Position

Warm-ups

When you manage to find
a moment to dedicate to
practising and creating beautiful
calligraphy, the first step is to
warm up.

Over the following 11 pages, I've
created some exercises to help
you to focus on getting the ink
flowing, shaping your lettering
and simply allowing your mind to
let go.

Concentrate on getting your
thick strokes thick and your
thin strokes thin – forget about
everything else! As you become
more practised, you'll be able to
use some of the shorter quotes
to warm up, rather than the
exercises. Go at least twice as
slowly than you would when
writing normally.

Patterns

Practising using patterns and
flourishes can be as beneficial as
letter drills – they're all shapes,
after all – so I've included
some fluid, swirling designs and
illustrations for you to trace. You'll
need to turn the book around
as you work, allowing you to get
your pen at the right angle to
make that downstroke thick on
the page.

These exercises are all about
training your muscle memory.
With time and practice, you'll
automatically put the pressure on
the downstroke and lift with the
upstroke, allowing your mind the
freedom to unwind, tune out and
simply get lost in the creativity.

YouTube
Kirsten Burke Calligraphy
Secrets – Thick and thins

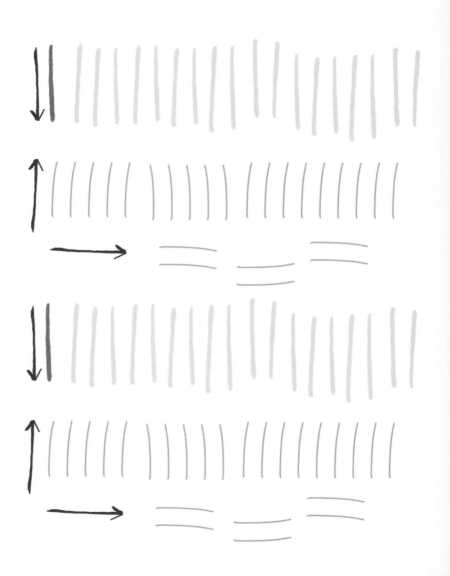

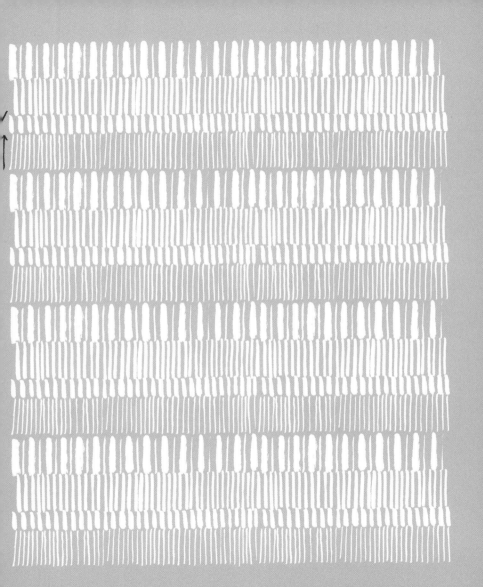

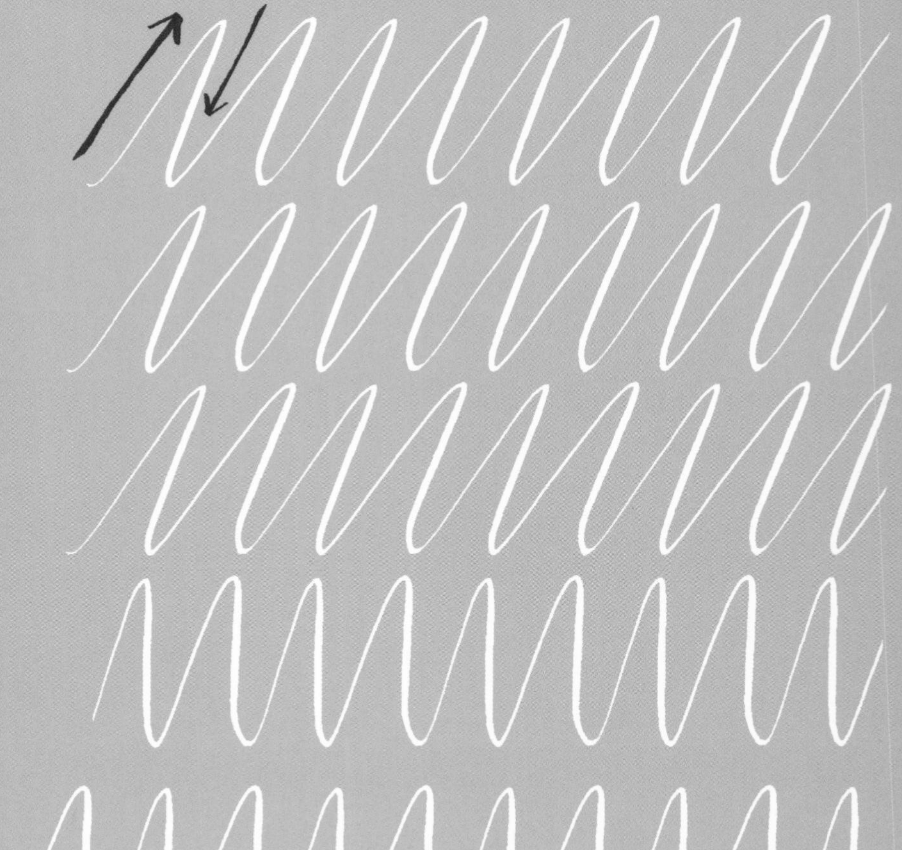

...and relax!

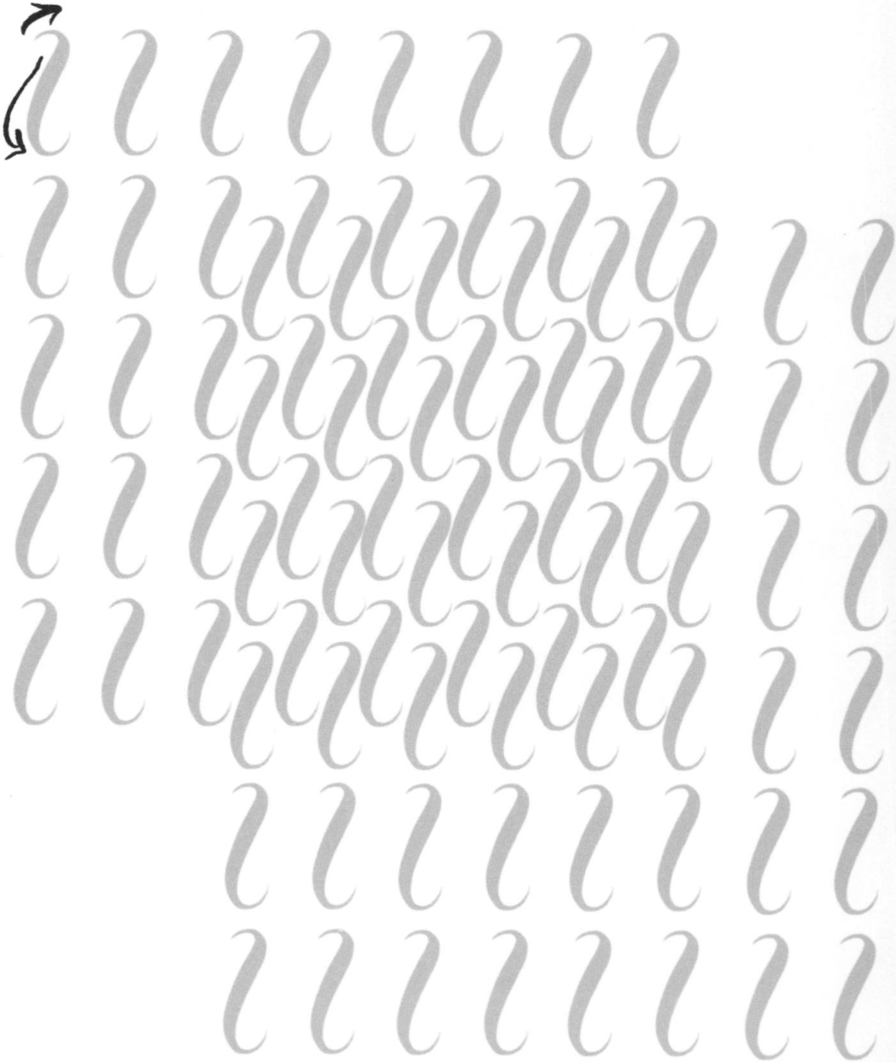

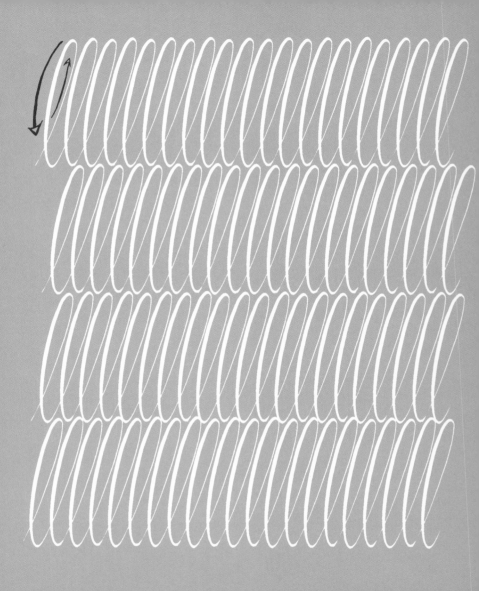

On these next three pages you'll need to 'puzzle' out the up and downstrokes! Turn the book around until your page and pen stroke are in the right position. Remember, a thick stroke is a downstroke and a thin stroke is an upstroke.

These designs can be used as
flourishes, to fill spaces, or to
add interest to other pieces.
Later on in the book you can
use this page as inspiration.

Quotes

In today's crazy world of juggling and self-judgement, positive mantras are a powerful tool, quieting the mental chatter that can affect our self-belief. Here's a selection of my favourite pick-me-up quotes and phrases to work with. I've given each a guide time to complete, so you can indulge your soulful side no matter how long you have. Simply choose the quote that reaches out to you at that moment.

Use your downtime moments, however fleeting, when the kettle is boiling or the bath is running. Choose a short quote and give *yourself* five minutes. You can do as many as you like at a time.

As you journey through the book and work through the exercises, you'll gain muscle memory. As your confidence increases, have a go at the challenge pages, where you can add additional levels of skill to the exercises.

Some of these pages have a blue or green colour wash on them, so use bright inks in contrasting colours or shimmering metallics, so that your lettering 'pops' out against the wash.

Relax as you trace, shape and create the lines, strokes and imagery, creating something with your hands. Being truly creative helps to reduce stress and improves our well-being. Take a moment and enjoy.

YouTube
Kirsten Burke Calligraphy
Secrets – Ink Flow

Modern Italic Alphabet

Use this as a guide as you work through the quotes. Follow the numbers and arrows denoting the stroke order and direction. Thick strokes are downstrokes, thin strokes are upstrokes. Most cross strokes are also thin.

the Beginning is Always TODAY

MARY SHELLEY

Relax nothing is in Control

BUDDHA

Relax
nothing
IS IN
Control
BUDDHA

YouTube
Kirsten Burke Calligraphy
Secrets – Bounce

 or

Challenge for 30-minute focus

Trace over this quote using a contrasting colour for the word
'breathe'. The letters are 'knitted together' and move up and down,
rather than being in a straight line. This is called 'bounce'. Try
different colours on the next page.

Go it Alone

Troubleshooting

Avoiding a sagging bottom!
Concentrate on getting the position of
the thick stroke on the side of the letter
shape. Don't let that thick line drop and
hang at the bottom. To join up the 'o'
to the next letter, go all the way round
to the top, then you can use a small
loop through the 'o', followed by a thin
upwards stroke as shown below.

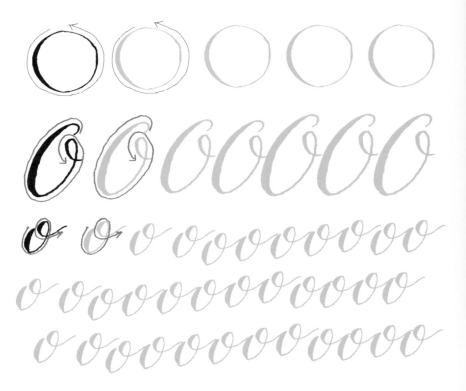

Failure
Failure
Failure
IS
success
IN
Progress

ALBERT
EINSTEIN

Hello
Weekend

10-minute time out

every
smile
makes you
a day
younger

CHINESE PROVERB

 or ## Challenge for 30-minute focus

Add flourishes. Work in pencil, then ink, perhaps in a different colour so that the flourish stands out. Take care that twirls don't look like letters!

It's never too late to follow your DREAMS and there's no time like the present to start

ANONYMOUS

Because of you,
I laugh
a little harder,
cry a little less,
& smile
a lot more

10-minute time out

Be the energy
you want to
attract

 or ## Challenge for 30-minute focus

Cover up a section of this page then gently tap a small paintbrush with some ink on it over the part that's showing to create sprinkles over your work. This technique can really bring a piece to life and is a great cover-up for accidents!

Go it Alone

Troubleshooting

Adding a flourish

Flourishes are a great way to add fun to a piece. They can also work brilliantly to fill a space and balance your work. Take care not to make a word difficult to read because of a flourish that you've added. It's easy to make a shape that reads as a letter. See how the flourishes here could be mistaken for 'e' or 's'?

Flourishing comes from the larger movements of the arm, not the wrist, so keep your arm locked and steady. Add pressure when you go across if you want to add some thickness.

Perfectly Imperfect

Anyone who never
made a mistake
never tried
anything new

ALBERT EINSTEIN

Life is the most wonderful fairytale

HANS CHRISTIAN ANDERSEN

Take 5

make time for...

 Challenge for 30-minute focus

Finish off this quote with a word or two of your choice - it could be chocolate or wine! You may like to write the words in pencil first.

Happiness
never
decreases
by being
shared

BUDDHA

Good THINGS TAKE Time

You can
never cross
the ocean
until
you have
the courage
to lose
sight of
the shore

CHRISTOPHER COLUMBUS

You can never cross the ocean until you have the courage to lose sight of the shore

CHRISTOPHER COLUMBUS

keep your
face always
towards the
sunshine
+ SHADOWS
will fall
behind you

walt whitman

 or ## Challenge for 30-minute focus

Work in black, just to the side of the letters to create a shadow.
Go slowly, especially on the upstrokes, and don't cover the
lines. Then try a different light/dark combination opposite. This
technique is called 'shadowing'.

Go it Alone

Troubleshooting

Below is a colour wheel. Blend colours next to each other like yellow and blue, or red and blue, and you'll get a third colour. Blend colours that are opposite each other and you tend to get a murky brown.

Blending

To blend colours together so that your lettering merges from one colour to another, take two pots of coloured ink. Think about the colour they make if you mix them. Dip the nib into the first pot of ink and once that ink runs out, dip straight into the other colour. A drop or two of the first colour may go into the second pot, so if you want to avoid this happening, touch your nib on your napkin before you swap! Continue with your calligraphy, starting with the new colour from just before where you left off, so that you go over the last stroke that you were making. The colours run into each other because they're still wet, which gives a gorgeous effect.

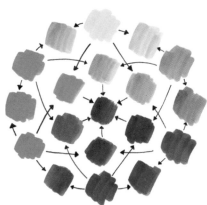

Red and blue creates purple.

Red and yellow creates orange.

Blue and green creates teal.

Work with a smooth, rhythmic movement. Don't rush. Paint each letter a stroke at a time. Experiment and have fun. You'll quickly learn what colours do and don't work.

YouTube
Kirsten Burke Calligraphy
Secrets – Dipping

I FOLLOWED MY & HEART it LED ME to the BEACH

NOTHING Great in the world has ever been accomplished without passion

GEORG WILHELM
FRIEDRICH HEGEL

A Good
laugh
is
SUNSHINE
in the
HOUSE

WILLIAM MAKEPEACE THACKERAY

The power
of imagination
makes us
infinite
JOHN MUIR

 or ## Challenge for 30-minute focus

Practise your colour blending skills. Pick complimentary colours and dip from one to the other as you work through this quote. Hone your skills on the fish pattern opposite!

30-minute focus

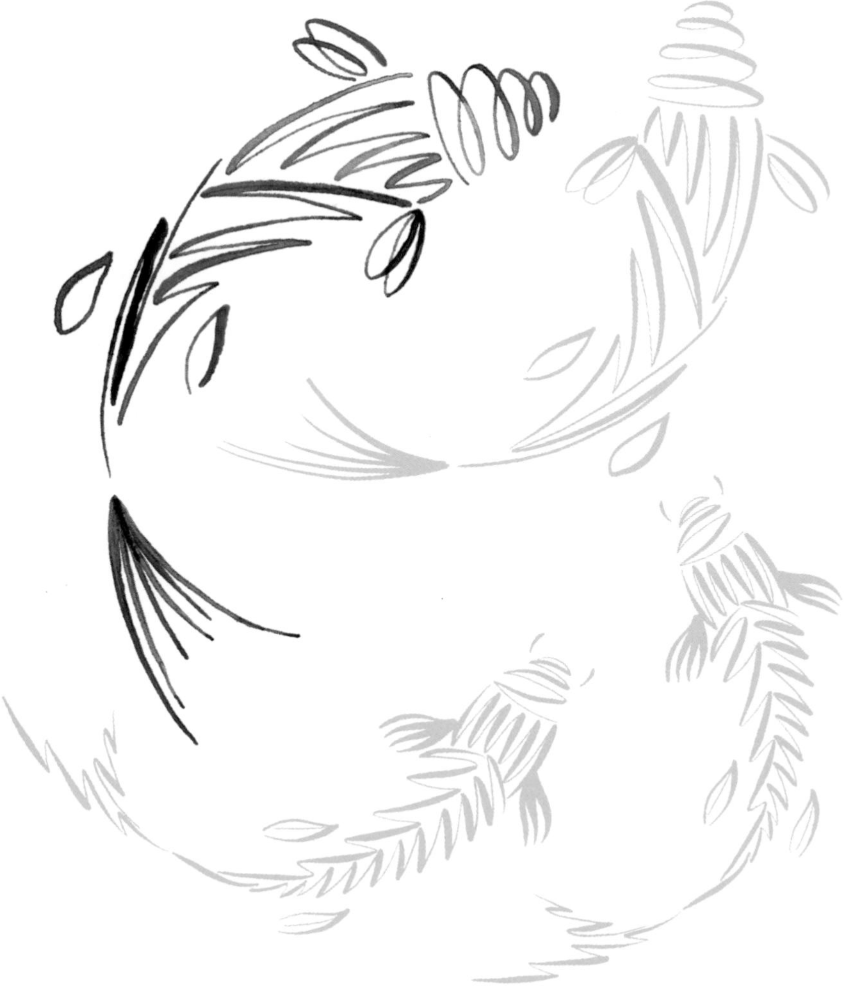

If you want to be HAPPY

BE

LEO TOLSTOY

The sight of THE stars ALWAYS makes me dream

VINCENT VAN GOGH

GREAT THINGS
are done by a
series of small
things
brought
together

VINCENT VAN GOGH

It is one of the Blessings of OLD Friends that you can afford TO BE Stupid with them

RALPH WALDO EMERSON

Go it Alone

Troubleshooting

Writing the letter S

Work over these 's' shapes, getting the contrast between your thick and thin lines. 'S' is a tricky letter, but there's no need to be afraid of it! Looking at the proportions of the roman capital 's' can help. Think about the curves going around two ovals. The modern version is the same, but you can play with the size of the ovals.

A smooth
SEA
never made
a skilled
SAILOR

FRANKLIN. D. ROOSEVELT

10-minute time out

Calm Calm
Calm Calm
Calm Calm
Calm Calm
Calm Calm

DOWN

IT ISN'T
WHAT WE
SAY
OR
THINK
THAT
defines
US BUT
what we
DO

JANE AUSTEN

The smallest act of kindness is worth MORE than the GRANDEST intention

OSCAR WILDE

 Challenge for 30-minute focus

Draw a border to connect these hearts – either a simple rectangle or lots of flourishes and twirls. Work in pencil first, then ink over it.

A beautiful thing

IS NEVER

perfect

EGYPTIAN PROVERB

All the flowers of all the tomorrows are in the seeds of today

INDIAN PROVERB

With freedom, books, flowers, and the moon, who could not be happy?

OSCAR WILDE

Be Happy for this MOMENT
THIS MOMENT is your LIFE

OMAR KHAYYAM

Go it Alone

Troubleshooting

Forming your letters

A common misconception is that the shapes that make up each letter are 'bolted' togeth In fact, each letterform moves up and down, like a zig-zag. By breaking down the letters below, it's clearer how the loop of an 'a' moves up to the top of the letter shape before dropping down.

connection

connection

The same is true in reverse with a 'b' shape. The loop starts at the bottom, going up and back down, joining again at the bottom.

I have been
bent & broken
but I hope into a
better shape

Charles Dickens
Great Expectations

Every Adventure requires a First Step

THE CHESHIRE CAT

ALL WE NEED
to be really
HAPPY
something IS
ENTHUSIASTIC TO BE
ABOUT

CHARLES KINGSLEY

HAPPINESS
is a butterfly
which
when pursued
is always
BEYOND our
grasp but
which if you
sit quietly
may alight
UPON you

NATHANIEL HAWTHORNE

(**or**) **Challenge for 30-minute focus**

Add some extra illustrations like butterflies or flowers and
flourishes around this quote.

blue sky,
ocean breeze
sun-kissed nose
& sandy toes

life's a beach!

I would ALWAYS rather be HAPPY than dignified

Charlotte Brontë

Believe
YOU
CAN
+ you're
½ WAY THERE

THEODORE ROOSEVELT

Believe YOU CAN + you're 1/2 WAY THERE

THEODORE ROOSEVELT

Take 5

Summer is a state of mind

 or ## Challenge for 30-minute focus

Add flourishes. Work in pencil first, then ink. Highlight your flourishes with a different colour. Take care that swirls don't look like letters!

Go it Alone

Troubleshooting

If you're still struggling to get a nice thick downstroke, the nib might be slightly tipped to one side, which will mean the tines cannot open.

Try a slight change in the angle of the page. You'll be surprised how the slightest alteration can make all the difference.

Aim for the tines to touch the paper equally, and for your downwards line to feel smooth and not scratchy.

— **Tines**

Geting the pressure right

If you feel there isn't enough contrast between your thick and thins, spend a moment concentrating on the pressure you're applying. Unlike handwriting, calligraphy requires a complete adjustment from that heavy downstroke, to the light-as-a-feather upstroke. Don't be afraid to apply some pressure. The nib is designed for that purpose. The wider the tines split open, the thicker your line will be.

Try practising adding pressure on your downstroke to the next quote – make those thick strokes really chunky!

 Challenge for 30-minute focus

Try doubling up on the downstrokes. Make a second downstroke next to the one printed leaving a small strip of white space, nib width, in between the two. Start doing this on all the capitals, then decide if you need to add in more to balance your piece.

by the Sea
all worries
wash away

Keep your eyes on the STARS & your feet on the ground

THEODORE ROOSEVELT

What lies behind us
& what lies before us
are tiny matters
compared to what lies
WITHIN US

RALPH WALDO EMERSON

Take 5

Out
of
Office

Happiness often sneaks in through a door you didn't know you left open

John Barrymore

The true sign of intelligence is not KNOWLEDGE but imagination

ALBERT EINSTEIN

The true Sign OF intelligence IS NOT KNOWLEDGE BUT imagination

ALBERT EINSTEIN

15-minute chill-out

MAKE THE best use of WHAT IS IN your POWER & TAKE THE rest as it HAPPENS

EPICTETUS

 Challenge for 30-minute focus

Highlights mimic the effect of light 'bouncing' off the letters. Add a short thin 'highlight' line to the capitals over the downstroke in the middle. Follow the shape of the letter. A short line and a dot underneath also works. This is called 'stippling'.

Go it Alone

Troubleshooting

Adding some bling

Metallic inks can separate, so Coliro have come to calligraphers' rescue with their range of shimmering watercolours. Mix as you would paints, to the consistency of single cream, then apply to the underneath of your nib with a brush.

YouTube
Kirsten Burke Calligraphy
Secrets – Finetec

Life is really simple but we insist on making it complicated

CONFUCIUS

Life's roughest storms prove the strength of our anchors

UNKNOWN

make time for yourself make time for yourself make time for yourself

the best way to predict your FUTURE is to create it

ABRAHAM LINCOLN

 or ## Challenge for 30-minute focus

Before you start tracing, use two different colour highlighter pens to make a futuristic stripey background on this artwork. This technique also works with pencil or pale felt pens.

Simplicity
IS THE ULTIMATE
SOPHISTICATION

LEONARDO DA VINCI

A Garden to walk in & immensity to dream in what more could he ask? A few flowers at his feet & above him the stars

VICTOR HUGO

the darker the path the brighter your light can shine

 or ## Challenge for 30-minute focus

Combine your skills. Use colour-blended metallics. Dip between colour and metallic ink to get shimmering results!

Start by doing what's necessary, then do what's possible & suddenly you are doing the impossible

ST FRANCIS OF ASSISI

It is NEVER too LATE to be what YOU might have BEEN

GEORGE ELIOT

MAGIC is believing in yourself if you can do that you can make anything HAPPEN

JOHANN WOLFGANG VON GOETHE

There is nothing better than a FRIEND... unless it is a friend with CHOCOLATE

CHARLES DICKENS

Live in the
sunshine
swim the sea
drink the
wild air

RALPH WALDO EMERSON

What you
think you
become

What you
feel you
attract

What you
imagine
you create

BUDDHA

To Sum Up

I hope this book has helped you to find moments to be still, mindful and absorbed in something creative and that, through calligraphy, you've found a means of escape.

In concentration and focus, you can let go of some of the tensions that dominate life – even if just for a moment – as you concentrate on perfecting those thick and thin lines, absorbed in the words, inspired and calmed by the positive mantras on each page.

Through these exercises, you've gained muscle memory and improved your skills, so make sure you continue to take time out and practise, even for just five minutes.

About us

I can hardly believe I've been a professional calligrapher for more than 20 years. After qualifying with a degree in graphic design, I completed a postgrad course in traditional calligraphy, illuminated lettering, gilding and bookbinding. I learned how to create the most exquisitely perfect lettering, which was painstaking and precise, but what I loved most was experimentation, making bold, vibrant contemporary artworks and making pictures out of words.

Back in 1997, I set up The Modern Calligraphy Company from a studio in Deptford with my friend, Jill. She looked after the business, leaving me free to be creative. We saw the decorative opportunity with calligraphy and set about showcasing designs on everything from greetings cards to windows for restaurants, museums, galleries and luxury brands nationwide.

I love experimenting with new tools. One day I'll be working with a 'cola pen' (a pen made out of a can of coke) and neon UV paints, then the next day I'll be using embossing powders and heat guns to create raised metallics on glass! Calligraphy connects the ancient with the modern, and technology has given it the opportunity to transform, stay relevant and reinvent itself.

Calligraphy has never been more exciting. I'm fortunate to work on a range of fascinating commissions, and train new apprentices from across the globe. But my first love will always be sharing the versatility of calligraphy and nurturing peoples' own love of lettering to see where that journey takes them.

About The Modern Calligraphy Company

The Modern Calligraphy Company is now the best-trusted calligraphy company in the UK, and we have more than 70 calligraphers working for our network. The last few years have been an exciting time of growth and hard work, as the cultural shift towards creative hobbies and mindfulness activities increased the popularity of calligraphy. As demand grew, so did we. You can now book a workshop in one of our many locations nationwide, knowing that you'll get our excellent content with 20 years of experience behind it.

In 2020, like many other small businesses, we adapted to new ways of keeping in touch with our customers. We launched our Live Stream workshops, which have been a huge success. We're now able to teach people in all sorts of places, including internationally!

As well as running our workshops, we are still working with luxury brands to create custom designs and bespoke packaging, and are running our online shop, which stocks the lastest calligraphy supplies.

We're so grateful to all of our customers and followers for their constant excitement, enthusiasm and encouragement, and we hope that we are able to give that back to them as we share our passion for creating beautiful calligraphy in new and exciting ways.

Supplies

With modern calligraphy becoming more popular by the day, many more products can be obtained from high-street and online retailers.

Nibs

It can be hard to know which nibs to buy, as they can all look the same, so I've put together an 'essentials kit' that includes three different nibs. Most people in my workshops find these the easiest nibs to use. It also contains a penholder and ink in a handy storage tin.

Brush pens

Our favourite is the 'Kirsten Burke Sailor' dual tip black pen. It has two sizes of brush, so you only need to pack one pen to create different-sized lettering.

Amazon and **Etsy** stock all of our products, so go to either site and search for Kirsten Burke Calligraphy, or you can buy direct from our website: www.kirstenburke.co.uk.

YouTube: Kirsten Burke The Modern Calligraphy Co
Instagram: themoderncalligraphyco
Twitter: kirstenburkeart
Facebook: The Modern Calligraphy Co.
Pinterest: The Modern Calligraphy Co.
www.themoderncalligraphyco.com

A STUDIO PRESS BOOKS

First published in the UK in 2018 by Studio Press,
an imprint of Bonnier Books UK,
The Plaza, 535 King's Road, London, SW10 0SZ
Owned by Bonnier Books,
Sveavägen 56, Stockholm, Sweden

www.studiopressbooks.co.uk
www.bonnierbooks.co.uk

3 5 7 9 10 8 6 4 2

By Kirsten Burke and Jill Hembling
Photography by Stewart Grant and Jason Hedges
Video Production by Flutterby Films
Edited by Kirsty Walters

Printed in China

An extra special 'thank you' to Maisie Minett who has helped to create
and test the calligraphy included in the book and to Felicity Barnes
for her wonderful way with words!

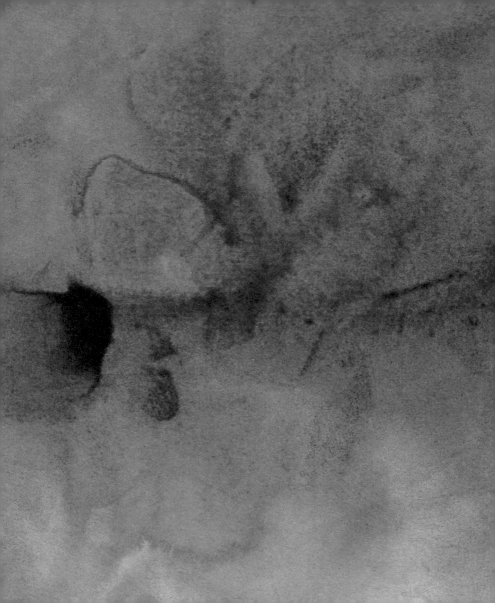